MY CALENDAR

NAME

5 7

PASTE HERE

PASTE HERE

CAMP BUS

SO-DLE-966

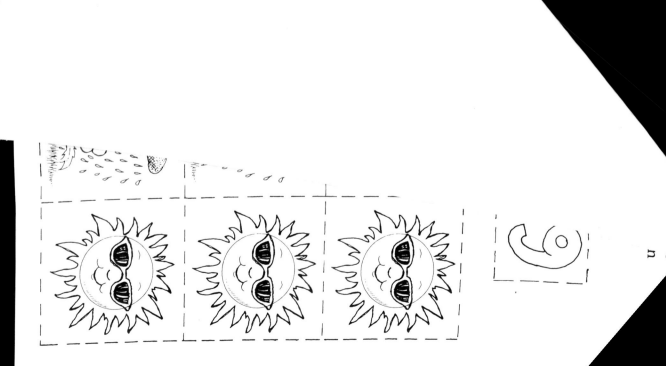

We have our own special way of counting time. There are 12 Hebrew months. Every time you see a new moon in the sky, it is the beginning of a new Hebrew month. The beginning of each Hebrew month is called ROSH HODESH. Use these stickers to mark ROSH HODESH for each month on your calendar. Then number the rest of the days in the month. (ROSH HODESH is the 1st day—number 1).

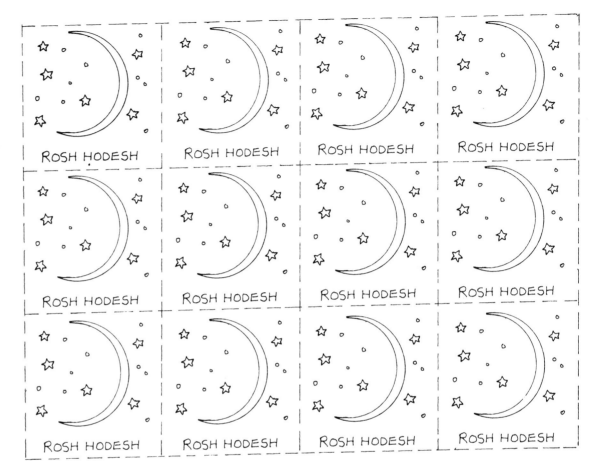

Every two or three years we have a LEAP YEAR. On each leap year we add a whole extra month. The extra month is called Adar Sheni. If this is a LEAP YEAR, copy the Adar month page in your calendar and paste this sticker on the gragger to make the 13th month.

ADAR SHENI
אֲדָר שֵׁנִי

A holiday is a special day. Most holidays come only once a year. But there is one holiday we have every week. It comes every Saturday. It is called the Sabbath — SHABBAT, in Hebrew. We eat a Sabbath meal. We light candles. We sing Kiddush and we eat hallah. We go to the synagogue and pray and listen as the Torah is read out loud. SHABBAT is a gift from God. It is a gift of one special day in every week, every week of the year. Each month, mark every SHABBAT on your calendar. There are lots of stickers because there are many Sabbaths in the year. *Shabbat Shalom!*

SHABBAT SHABBAT SHABBAT

SHABBAT SHABBAT SHABBAT

SHABBAT SHABBAT SHABBAT SHABBAT SHABBAT SHABBAT

SHABBAT SHABBAT SHABBAT SHABBAT SHABBAT SHABBAT

SHABBAT SHABBAT SHABBAT SHABBAT SHABBAT SHABBAT

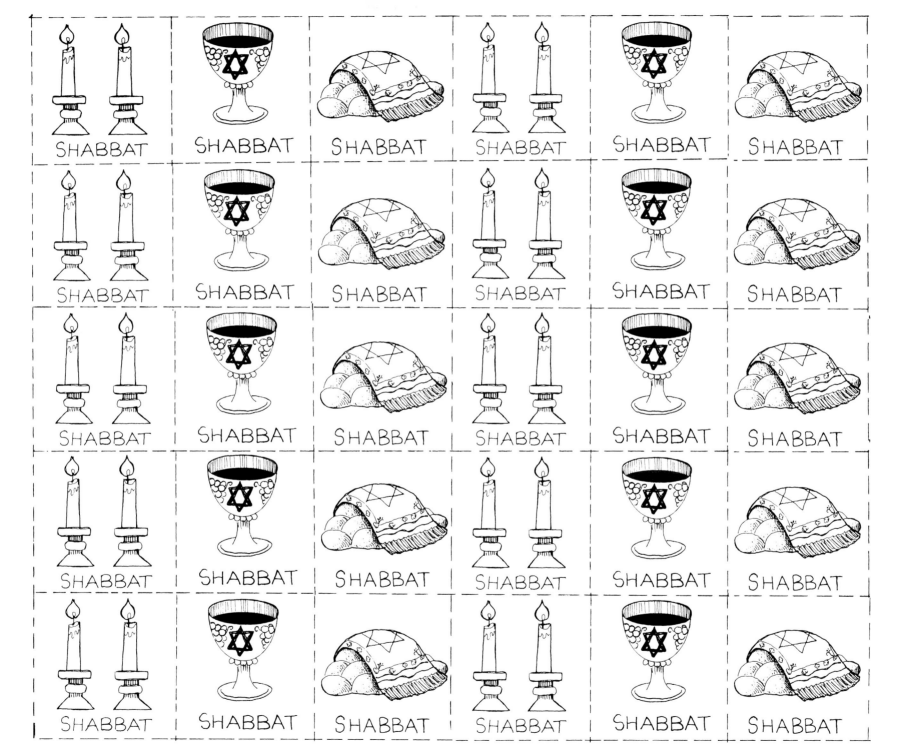

SHABBAT	SHABBAT	SHABBAT	SHABBAT	SHABBAT	SHABBAT
SHABBAT	SHABBAT	SHABBAT	SHABBAT	SHABBAT	SHABBAT
SHABBAT	SHABBAT	SHABBAT	SHABBAT	SHABBAT	SHABBAT
SHABBAT	SHABBAT	SHABBAT	SHABBAT	SHABBAT	SHABBAT
SHABBAT	SHABBAT	SHABBAT	SHABBAT	SHABBAT	SHABBAT

Tishray is the first Hebrew month. ROSH HASHANAH is the first day in the first month. ROSH HASHANAH is the Jewish New Year. It is the birthday of the world. We blow the shofar and we pray for a good year. We eat apples dipped in honey. Many Jews celebrate ROSH HASHANAH for two days. Use the sticker(s) to mark the beginning of the Jewish year on your calendar. *May God write you down for a good and sweet year.*

YOM KIPPUR is a very holy day. It comes 10 days after Rosh Hashanah. On YOM KIPPUR we are sorry for the bad things we have done. We ask God to forgive us. We ask our friends to forgive us too. Jews fast on YOM KIPPUR. Synagogue services on YOM KIPPUR are the most important of the year and they are the longest too. Count the 10 days carefully, beginning with Rosh Hashanah, and mark your calendar with the YOM KIPPUR sticker.

The Festival of SUKKOT comes in the fall, in the month of Tishre, on the 15th day. SUKKOT celebrates harvest time. SUKKOT means "booths" or "huts." We build a sukkah outdoors. We hang fruits and vegetables on it. We eat in the sukkah and we have parties in it. The SUKKOT holiday lasts for 7 days. Mark the 7 days of SUKKOT on your calendar.

The 8th day of Sukkot has its own name. It is called SHEMINI ATZERET. We pray for rain on this day. Mark your calendar with the sticker.

SIMHAT TORAH comes the day after Sukkot. We finish reading the Torah on SIMHAT TORAH. As soon as we finish, we start to read the Torah all over again. We make sure to remember God's teachings. It is a time for dancing and singing. It may be the happiest holiday in the whole year. Mark SIMHAT TORAH on your calendar.

HANUKKAH begins on the 25th day of the month of Kislev. HANUKKAH is called the Festival of Lights. We celebrate it by lighting candles for 8 nights. On each night we add another candle. We sing songs and we eat *latkes,* potato pancakes. We give gifts and we also play a HANUKKAH game. We spin a *draydel,* a top. Mark the 8 nights of HANUKKAH on your calendar.

On TU BI-SHEVAT we celebrate the New Year for the Trees. We send money to the Jewish National Fund for tree planting in Israel. TU BI-SHEVAT means "the 15th day of the month of Shevat." Mark TU BI-SHEVAT on your calendar and remember to plant a tree!

The 14th day of the month of Adar is the merriest day of the Jewish year. We celebrate the holiday of PURIM. We read the *Megillah* and use noisemakers called *graggers.* We dress up in costume and eat *hamantaschen.* Use the sticker to mark PURIM on your calendar.

Our PASSOVER holiday is celebrated for either 7 or 8 days. PASSOVER begins on the 15th day of the month of Nisan. We have a special dinner on the first night. It is called a Seder. We read the PASSOVER story from the Haggadah. We eat matzah every day during the holiday. Mark the days of PASSOVER on your calendar.

YOM HASHOAH is a day set aside to remember the Holocaust. It comes on the 27th day of the month of Nisan. We remind ourselves that sometimes people can be very evil to other people. Mark this sad day on your calendar.

YOM HA'ATZMA'UT is Israel's Independence Day. It is a new holiday. The Land of Israel is very old, but the State of Israel is new. Israel became a State in the year 1948. We are proud to have a Jewish State and we celebrate on the 5th day of the month of Iyar. Mark YOM HA'ATZMA'UT on your calendar.

We count the 49 days between the second day of Passover and the holiday of Shavuot. The 33rd day of the counting is a holiday. It is called LAG BA-OMER. It is a day for bows and arrows and picnics and hikes. It is a special day for schoolchildren. Mark your special day on the calendar.

On SHAVUOT we celebrate the day when the Israelites received the Ten Commandments at Mount Sinai. We decorate the synagogue with fruit and flowers. We eat foods made with milk and cheese. SHAVUOT means weeks. If you count 7 weeks (49 days) from the second day of Passover, you will find the holiday of SHAVUOT. We celebrate the holiday on the 6th day of the month of Sivan. Mark SHAVUOT on your calendar with the sticker.

We have many happy things to celebrate during the year, but we have some very terrible things to remember too. TISHA BE-AV is one of our saddest days. It comes on the 9th day of the month of Av. Long ago, on the 9th day of Av, the Temple of Jerusalem was burned to the ground. Mark this sad day on your calendar.

Birthdays are fun. You can celebrate Hebrew birthdays too! Find out the Hebrew date of your birthday and mark it on your calendar. Can you find out your parents' Hebrew birthdays and the Hebrew birthdays of your brothers and sisters? Mark them on your calendar too.

LAG BA-OMER

YOM HA'ATZMA'UT

YOM HASHOAH

NAME

TISHA BE-AV

SHAVUOT

NAME

NAME

NAME

NAME

NAME

NAME

TISHRE

תִּשְׁרֵי

SUNDAY	MONDAY	TUESDAY	WEDNESDAY	THURSDAY	FRIDAY	SHABBAT

SUNDAY	MONDAY	TUESDAY	WEDNESDAY	THURSDAY	FRIDAY	SHABBAT

KISLEV

כִּסְלֵו

SUNDAY	MONDAY	TUESDAY	WEDNESDAY	THURSDAY	FRIDAY	SHABBAT

TEVET

טֵבֵת

SUNDAY	MONDAY	TUESDAY	WEDNESDAY	THURSDAY	FRIDAY	SHABBAT

THIS TREE HAS BEEN PLANTED IN ISRAEL IN HONOR OF

SHEVAT

שְׁבָט

SUNDAY	MONDAY	TUESDAY	WEDNESDAY	THURSDAY	FRIDAY	SHABBAT

SUNDAY	MONDAY	TUESDAY	WEDNESDAY	THURSDAY	FRIDAY	SHABBAT

NISAN
נִיסָן

SUNDAY	MONDAY	TUESDAY	WEDNESDAY	THURSDAY	FRIDAY	SHABBAT

SUNDAY	MONDAY	TUESDAY	WEDNESDAY	THURSDAY	FRIDAY	SHABBAT

SIVAN

סִיוָן

SUNDAY	MONDAY	TUESDAY	WEDNESDAY	THURSDAY	FRIDAY	SHABBAT

TAMMUZ
תַּמּוּז

SUNDAY	MONDAY	TUESDAY	WEDNESDAY	THURSDAY	FRIDAY	SHABBAT

AV

אָב

SUNDAY	MONDAY	TUESDAY	WEDNESDAY	THURSDAY	FRIDAY	SHABBAT

SUNDAY	MONDAY	TUESDAY	WEDNESDAY	THURSDAY	FRIDAY	SHABBAT